STILL LIVING

A VICTIMIZED MAN'S JOURNEY

MARCEL ANDERSON

Rain Publishing

KNIGHTDALE, NC

Marcel Anderson/Rain Publishing
PO Box 702
Knightdale, NC 27545
www.rainpublishing.com
www.marcelanderson.com

Front Cover Image/Design: Fredrick Giles with Strongbird Studios; Email: fred@strongbirdstudios.com

Book Cover Design and Layout: Trevis C. Bailey, www.SDCreativeWorks.com

Edited by: Rain Publishing, LLC www.RainPublishing.com

Ordering Information: Quantity sales. Special discounts are available on quantity purchases by corporations, associations, and others. For details, contact the "Special Sales Department" at the address above.

Still Living/ Marcel Anderson. —1st ed.
ISBN 978-0-9899742-7-1

Library of Congress: 2014936239

Praise for Marcel Anderson's

Still Living: A Victimized Man's Journey

"You will read about the unthinkable in this book and feel all types of emotions. Even though this book reads like a movie, it's a real life experience. Marcel is a survivor and what happened next is heroic. He retaliated but in a way that makes him a winner. Marcel is sharing his heart on a serious topic within our community and thousands will be changed by what is in this book. I'm looking forward to sharing this book and experiencing it on the big screen someday."

~Alphaeus Anderson, Founder of Stellar Award-Winning, Pure N Heart

"This book is a must-read for every man who has been victimized at the hands of another. Marcel tells his story with unmitigated detail and courageous transparency. He then shows the path to victory by marrying his challenging course with the unfailing love of Jesus, and the power of the gospel. He does not over-spiritualize the internal journey to wholeness. Marcel puts the process on the ground where true recovery is lived out day by day, among our families and community of faith. If he is man enough to write it, be man enough to read it. Do you want to be made whole?"

~B. McKinley Bayless

"*Still Living* will change how people look at assault and abuse. Marcel has been able to shed light on the paradigm shift by expressing his story in a riveting way, but most importantly, how he was able to overcome."
~Donald Anthony Wheeler

"Without hesitation this book reveals there is strength in truth. It will help men to be open about their deepest pain. He let us know, the greater the pain, the greater the man."
~Minister Eddie Parks, Associate Minister,
First Baptist Church of Fairforest, Spartanburg, SC

"Marcel Anderson has written a book of such courage and inner strength it could only be the Spirit inspiring it. At times light and comical, at other times excruciating, *Still Living* will put your tragedies and triumphs in perspective and inspire you to an ever closer and more honest relationship with God than you thought you could enjoy. After all, if Marcel Anderson can come away still living and still loving God, you'll know you can too. *Still Living* is the bravest book I've ever read."
~Pastor Maurice Wallace,
Cornerstone Community Church, Durham, NC

"With overflowing insights about us as a people, Anderson helps readers take that first step toward fruitful change."
~Dr. Tony Warrick

This Book is dedicated to

Dr. Aaron T. Anderson
aka Mr. Table Talk

CONTENTS

CONTENTS

Acknowledgments

Who else would get my first thank you in this book? God is my everything, even when I need Him the most. He's the strength of my life and without Him I couldn't allow myself to push through this writing journey. My path of self-discovery happened because of Him breathing His Word into me before the foundations of the earth and I thank Him for giving me this opportunity to share His message of Love. This is something new and I can't help but cherish the moment of learning more about who I really am as a Man.

I thank my mother Altie Anderson who encouraged me ever since I was in the 2nd grade to keep moving forward. "Don't let a teacher's comment hold you down," she told me. She inspired me to speak publicly, and she challenged me spiritually when I was growing up. Today I can see how it helped me gain confidence in the Lord. My mother had so much to give all of her children, but most of all she gave us love that could never be broken.

Thanks to my father Dewayne Anderson (AKA) Big Noise, for giving us the opportunity to see what it means to work for yourself and implementing the entrepreneurial spirit in my life. "Become your own boss," were his words. "But you will always have a boss, even when you work for yourself." I definitely understand what that means now. He gave me advice to never take too much from anyone, to speak up and speak clearly "so they can hear you." He worked hard and, "Money doesn't grow on trees" was his motto. He also taught me the importance of crawling before walking. I never really understood what that meant until I became older.

To my oldest sister Sonya, thanks for leading the way with your encouraging words. Thanks Joe for being by her side.

Thanks to my sister Kim, the sister that everybody can see, the sister who listens when we have so much to talk about.

To Ursula, the third youngest of all my sisters: thanks for staying tough and strong and showing tough love when we need it.

Thank you to my brother Alphaeus and his wife Alexias. Dude, you push me to never stop what I believe in. From the musical sessions and discussions about business moves, they are all valuable conversations. *He's a Heale*r is a song that will bless so many, thanks Alphaeus for putting your anointing on it. God is still in the healing business.

Thanks to my twin brother Marcus. It's been a journey working on my cd and now presenting my first book. It's been a long time coming. There is nothing like seeing your hard work pay off. Thanks for pushing me to write deeper. We constantly help each other get to that next place in life and that's what it means to have a positive, supportive twin brother. Keep playing the sax.

To my aunts and uncles, and everyone who plays a part in my life, I thank you for helping me get to that special place in life.

To Aunt Sarah and Uncle Nigel, on numerous occasions you guys have been very inspirational by your example without saying anything. Uncle Nigel, your weekly motivational moments have helped me see greater potential within myself. Thanks for your words and books, I'm still reading them.

Thanks Anthony and Shavon Wheeler for your encouraging words and the books you sent me to read. You help show me another way - the right way to do it yourself. Having your own business is very possible if you just work hard and keep at it.

Thanks to my church family, First Baptist Church of Fairforest and Pastor Jenkins who leads them in worship on Sunday mornings. Thanks for your continued prayers and blessings.

To Minister Parks, thanks for helping me strengthen my spiritual walk in God. You have served as one of my good mentors in the Gospel.

Pastor Bayless, you gave me the opportunity to become a licensed minster and today I'm able to share the Good News of Jesus Christ because of some of your teachings.

Thanks to Dr. Maurice Wallace and his wife Pamela for allowing me to connect at Cornerstone.

Dr. Tony Warrick and Ashely, I want to say thank you for helping me get through some tough times in this process. Your prayers and support were very much needed.

A special thanks to Amy N. Brock. Your constant support throughout this journey has been so great. Thanks for your loving prayers and tough advice. I truly cherish it all.

To some of my long-time family friends I grew up with and went to college with, thanks to Ryan, Josh, Randy, Alvin, Brent, Jossalyn, Darryl, Tony, Camille, Levar, Katie, Jason, Jamila, Melinda, Rod, Scott, Carl Wright, Dr. Washington, Mitch, Brandon, Dr. William Logan, Kelsy Lodge, Timothy Eaton, Josh, Steve, Missy, Jr. Wheeler, Aunt Bob, Uncle Donnie, Uncle Ricky, Uncle James, Ricky, Miesha, Latoya, Beverly, Cynt, Aisha, Teresa, Little Donald, Laron, Will Artis, and so many I can't name them.

To my high school mentor and coach, Wendy Barr: you helped me write some long papers. I know God sent you to help me through my high school journey. Thank you.

To all of the brothers of Kappa Alpha Psi Fraternity Inc., thanks for being a supporting brotherhood.

To every staff member of Accelerating Men, Inc., thanks for helping to get this mentorship organization off the ground. I can't conduct our ETC workshops without you. Min. Laverne Richardson, Jeremy Holman, Delvin Gist, and Jeff Smith, you guys are the greatest team.

Thanks to Lawrence Rush and Fervent Love Media for helping me with some of my musical journey.

To Rain Publishing: without you this journey wouldn't have started. Thanks so much for the long hours in developing the finished product of this book. Jeff and Rachel Smith, God definitely has His Hands on you both.

Dr. Aaron T. Anderson, this book is dedicated to you man. Thanks for being a positive role model in my life.

Thanks to everyone who invested their time in me. If you are reading this book, I want to thank you for taking the time out to read it. Without your empowering support I couldn't have made it through this process. If I left someone out, please add your name here. I thank _____for your support.

Introduction

Looking back over my life, I never thought a day like this would come. I am moving forward and going to a place I've never been before. Writing a book wasn't something I thought I had time for. Let's just say life happens and changes are made during your journey. It's sometimes difficult to see yourself doing something new until it actually happens and that's how it was with me. I spoke of writing a book about what happened to me for so long but I never followed through until the right moment presented itself. When that moment arrived, I knew it was an opportunity for me to share my story. By listening to God first and connecting to the right people, I was preparing for my life to be revealed to a larger audience besides my immediate family.

Writing this book was a release for me and I constantly prayed that others within this community would listen to my voice. This book is for people who share some of the same experiences that I've had. If you have been sexually assaulted or abused by someone you know or don't know, this book is for you. If you have been keeping secrets about your personal experience, this book will help you gain the confidence to speak up. Here is a question you need to ask yourself: "Do I need to talk about my situation?"

I believe that everyone can benefit from reading this book because we have all experienced something in our lives that no one knows about. I don't know what you've been through, but I know that what you have experienced could help someone else get through their situation.

When I contemplated writing this book, I deeply considered why it was important to tell my story, and here I am. I'm starting a conversation about me, what happened to me, and why others should think about what they have gone through. I want to help others understand that life is not over if you are still living or breathing. Today is a new day and you have the chance to make a difference in another person's life if you speak up. Don't be afraid of what others may say about you. God has your back.

I pray that as you read this book, you will gain additional confidence in who God has designed and created you to be. In the midst of all of your adversity and challenges, I encourage you to keep going and be driven by your purpose. Through identifying and understanding your true purpose, you will find security. As you read through each chapter, I hope your mind and heart will be open to what my experience was and how God allowed me to make it through the most difficult moments of my life. Through His grace and mercy, you can find safety no matter what happens in your life.

CHAPTER ONE

GROWING UP ON THE FREY LINE

I was born and raised in Spartanburg, South Carolina on Frey Road, otherwise known as Frey Line, a place where I grew up with my three brothers, three sisters, and my distant cousins.

There was never a dull moment where I grew up. On Frey Line I used to play baseball, basketball, and football in the street, while some kids jumped rope and played hop scotch. That was my neighborhood, a place where I started developing some of my many gifts and talents. These talents would one day help me get to the next level in life.

Surrounded by people who loved me, my upbringing was about family staying together. Even when we got on each other's nerves, we stayed close and helped each other out. Sometimes we even fought over who would eat the last bit of spaghetti that my mother cooked. My

God, that's my family. I grew up with a big family where every year we would have a huge Fourth of July cookout and Christmas gathering with over 75-plus family members in one house.

I can never forget about the good days with family. That's what made me who I am today. Ever since I was a young boy I knew I was destined to do more with my life because my family told me I would. When I was a little boy, my mother always told me that she thought I was reincarnated because she saw me do things that she knew I couldn't have learned. I wasn't exposed to some of the things I was displaying around the house, she said. At the time I wasn't sure what that meant, but after a while I learned that God truly had His hand on my life.

Actor and comedian were some of the things my family considered me to be when I was younger. I was always getting into something around the house and even at the family events, cracking jokes and always dressing up as a different character during the holidays. I wanted to make people laugh and enjoy life. Curious about life and what it was all about, I always wanted to know and do more. I was always involved in community activities.

Very active in the church, I found one of my many gifts which is singing gospel music. I remember the first time I sang in church. Lord was I nervous when I started singing, but when I opened my mouth and sang *Give us This Day*, I knew it was a good day. Ever since then, I knew singing was a talent God had given me. I constantly worked on my singing ability by joining the chorus in elementary, middle, and high school. Over the years I started to write songs and connect with my musical brothers to record them. Music has and will always be part of my life.

When I began working on my first album in 2010, I felt that my life was starting to move forward and things were really starting to shape up for me in a good way. I started writing down my visions and connected with like-minded individuals.

2010 was also the year where I had just begun to see the results of my hard work leading into that season of my life. I founded the Accelerating Men mentoring organization, I released my demo cd and I was being assigned a new leadership position as youth minister at my church. I was approaching 2011 full of the excitement and anticipation that these endeavors would lead me to another level that God called me to reach. Motivated and inspired by my dreams and visions, I knew that something good was happening. I started taking life a lot more seriously. I wanted more out of life and the only way that could happen was if I pursued what God had given me wholeheartedly. Never once did I look back at some of the many challenges I faced in my life.

A couple of months prior to the end of the year, I was run off the road as I was driving on the highway, but thank God I wasn't hurt or killed. I was steady unfolding some new possibilities for my life. It was just a good place for me, full of self-discovery and seeing the man that God intended me to become. As I prepared myself for the New Year, I knew all of my plans were going to be executed because I was ready.

I was excited for a big break in my life, but what happens when your dreams and visions are put on hold because you're caught off guard? What do you do then? At this point, I didn't think anything could make me hit the pause button on my dreams.

CHAPTER TWO

WHAT IF I DIE TODAY?

"But about the day or hour no one knows, not even the angels in heaven nor the Son, but only the Father."
Matthew 24: 36

January 1, 2011

It was a normal Sunday morning for me. I woke up early and as I began getting myself ready for church service, I started praying the day would go well for me. But for some reason on that Sunday I was feeling something different in the air and didn't know how to grab hold of it.

"I feel weird," I told my friend Randy.

"Why do you feel so weird, man?"

"It's just one of those feelings you get in your stomach. It's not a normal feeling. Plus, over the last day or two, I kept feeling something like a knot on my ear. I'm not sure what it is or where it came from. Today it feels like it has grown and it hurts really bad. See? "

"Man that knot is huge!"

"Yeah I know!"

"So what are you going to do about it?"

"I'm not sure yet, but it feels even worse than it looks. If I have to go to the doctor, I won't be too happy about it. I hate going to the doctor, but I know sometimes you have to go in order to get well.   I'm just worried that my insurance won't cover my hospital bill."

"Why do you say that?"

"I'm still waiting for my paperwork from the school system to go through for my lateral entry status as a teacher. In the meanwhile, I'm still working as a substitute teacher, but my insurance and licensure paperwork won't clear until sometime after the New Year and I don't know if I can wait. This knot is throbbing like it's coming out of my head. It feels like somebody is beating on my ear drum."

Once church was over, we drove back to Randy's house to eat. Yes sir, that chicken and Kool-Aid was good. After we ate that good food, Randy tried to convince me to go to the hospital to see about the knot on my ear but I hate hospitals.

I probably should have gone because I couldn't shake that weird feeling I had from earlier in the day. I said to Randy, "Man you know what, what if I died today? What would happen man? We never know the day we are going to die, and we need to be prepared. All I know is, if I die I want you to say some good things about my life."

These thoughts were so strong in my mind that I actually called my mother and shared with her my thoughts and feelings. I asked, "Mom, what if I die today?" I described how I wanted my entire funeral to be. I told her I want my twin brother Marcus to play, and I want to be dressed in all white. I also made sure to tell her "I love you," before we hung up.

My mother thought I was talking crazy. She told me not to talk like that, but I explained to her that life is real and you never know what could happen to you. She didn't like that and said she didn't want to hear anything else I had to say.

CHAPTER THREE

STILL LIVING

"Sitting there all alone, praying to the Lord, my fear is gone. Almost gone but I'm still here, the grace that God has brought me here...I'm still alive, I'm thankful to God that I'm still alive...haha" ~ from the song, *Still Living* by Marcel Anderson

I had plans that evening to help my coworker move in to her new place. She and I were not in a relationship but we flirted with each other and had connected twice physically in the past. We really didn't speak much to each other even though we worked together, so it was a little strange when over the Christmas break she asked me if I would help her move. She didn't seem to have anyone else, so I agreed to help her out of the kindness of my heart. I called her to confirm that she still wanted me to come, and she did.

It was almost time to leave and I needed Randy to drive me back to my house so I could meet her there, but Randy said, "Man, I don't feel good about this situation."

I said, "No, it's ok, we're friends, and I want to help her."

"I'm really not sure about this man, and I normally don't get these types of feelings. I'm not taking you."

I thought about how else I could get there, knowing that I made a promise to someone that I wanted to keep. Randy was very adamant about not wanting to take me because of how he felt. Actually his words were starting to get to me and I felt a little funny about it but I also felt like I needed to keep my word.

"So, is this what friends are for? This is how you would do me? You gonna make me walk? I wouldn't make you walk to help a friend move. When you commit to someone do you go back on your word?"

"I don't know, but I'm not taking you."

I felt like Randy was just being the same old Randy again. We talked about this for about five-ten minutes and I just kept getting on Randy's nerves asking and insisting that he take me because he was the only ride I had at the time. My coworker was coming to pick me up from my house and if I didn't make it back in time she wouldn't have anyone to help her move (or so I thought). Finally, Randy gave in to my request and drove me back to my house.

I went inside to change clothes, and I waited until my coworker came to pick me up. As we drove to her house, there wasn't much conversation outside of small talk about how the day was going and what she needed help with. Randy's words kept haunting me, and I still felt a little weird, like, "What am I doing here? Why am I the only one who can help her? We haven't even really been close or had real communication in a while." The whole thing seemed strange but I was so bent on being a man of my word that I followed through with it.

The sun was just going down when she and I got to her new place. When she opened the door it was dark inside and she didn't immediately turn the light on which I thought was strange. I said, "Are you going to turn a light on?" She went down the hallway and turned it on. As I entered, I didn't see any furniture to the left. I noticed a couple of things spread out, but about two minutes later, someone came out of the closet and started yelling, "Get Down! Get Down! What are ya'll doing in here? Get Down!"

She screamed and I suddenly had a gun pointed to my head. I quickly saw that the guy's face was covered by a black ski mask and he had a pole in his other hand. He started shoving me toward the back of the house as my coworker continued to scream like someone was hurting her. He kept yelling, "What are ya'll doing in here? What are ya'll doing in here?"

"I'm helping her move..."

"Shut up!"

He handcuffed me, blindfolded me, and shoved me in the bathroom. I could hear him going back and forth, in and out of the room. It sounded a little like he would go and mess with her, she would "scream," and then he would come back to check on me. I tried to move the blindfold on my face to get a good look at what was going on. I couldn't really see anything clearly, because the blindfold was so tight on my face. I could see movement but I couldn't see who or what it was.

I was in the bathroom for about 15 minutes and I could still hear them moving around. The guy continued to come back every so often to check on me, then he moved me to a back room. I could still see just a little bit. He told me that I must do whatever he told me to do and if I listen and follow his instructions I may walk away and live. Boy was I shaken by those words. All I could think about was doing exactly what he told me to do.

He pushed me onto the floor and kept questioning me trying to find out why we were there. He asked me if I had any money or anything else on me. I didn't have anything except my cellphone and he took that. I kept hearing noises that sounded like someone was banging on the walls and he would call out somebody else's name, playing as if there were two of them but I figured that it was just him. She continued screaming as if she was being molested. I couldn't see anything because I was on the floor, but the noises were loud enough for me to hear clearly. I was just praying that she was ok; I couldn't do anything about it.

During the time I was on the floor he started to beat the snot out of me with a pole and constantly kicked me in my back, basically like I was a dummy. He repeatedly spoke negative words towards me and made sure I felt the pain that he intended me to feel. He kicked me in the head and said, "If you ever tell anybody, I been to jail before, I am at home at the jail, I don't care. I don't know who you think you are." It felt like he was after something, and I was in his way of getting it. I couldn't understand why he was doing all of these things to me but I was forced to take it all.

All of a sudden, he started to forcefully pull my pants down and told me to spread my legs open. He had a pole and started penetrating me with it at least 20 times. "Oh God!" I said to myself, "I know this is not happening to me. What is this pain?" The pain was so bad that I had to hold my stomach in and try to brace myself to even receive it and he kept yelling at me to hold still. I thought it was over but it was like he suddenly got angry and began doing it again, probably 30 more times, except on this round it was like he used deadly force. I could literally hear my insides moving. I couldn't take it. I was screaming and I couldn't believe what was happening.

Even as I express this I don't understand how I made it. I was hurting to the point where I couldn't move. I just kept strong like, "I have to make it through. I don't care what he does to me I have to stay strong." I felt like even if I died, it was ok. I just knew I wasn't going to leave there. His gun hit my head, and I heard it move once or twice. At one point the gun hit my hand and he said, "You trying to pick up the gun?!" In that moment, I felt like I was going to die.

After that was over I felt numb. My body was in shock. I didn't know what to say or do. I just knew that my body was not going to be working properly after that situation. My adrenaline was rushing and all I could do was wait to be shot, beaten, or violated again with the pole.

At that moment I prayed that God would get me out of the situation. I didn't know if I would even leave that room. Not knowing the motives of my attacker, I just wanted to stay alive. Moments went by where no sounds were being made. I thought to myself, "either he is gone or he is waiting to see what my move will be."

"The thief's purpose is to steal and kill and destroy. My purpose is to give them a rich and satisfying life." John 10:10 (NLT)

CHAPTER FOUR

JACKRABBIT

My life was flashing before my eyes as I laid there on that floor. I thought about growing up as a little boy on Frey Line. Yeah, that was the place to be in the summertime. My mother would cook hotdogs and chili for the entire street. That is just her spirit of giving, which she did freely for all of the kids in the neighborhood. We were all close and half of us were cousins.

The kids in the neighborhood would always race one another and I would do my best to be in the mix, thinking I was faster than everybody. For some reason I thought I was very fast, but I didn't win every race. However, I started running and exercising daily to increase my speed and I became faster. 'Jackrabbit' is what they used to call me. Yeah, that was me all right. I would run everywhere until I became tired. Running was something I grew to love. I would always watch my oldest brother Aaron run and I wanted to be just as good as he was.

Steadily over the years I continued to practice hard, started running high school track and did well, which led to me receiving a scholarship to Voorhees College in the small town of Denmark, South Carolina. Later I transferred to Saint Augustine's University in Raleigh, North Carolina to run on another track scholarship. I was so ready to move into a track career until I got injured at a major track meet at UNC Chapel Hill. I fell over a hurdle and laid there stunned and amazed that I wouldn't be able to finish the race. Lord knows I wanted to move, but my body wouldn't let me because I strained something in my leg.

Falling from a hurdle is not a pretty sight. Just ask a true hurdler who has fallen before. I was lying on the ground hurting, waiting for someone to rescue me, but no one immediately came to my care. I just knew somebody was watching me and would help me get off the track because I was in pain and I wasn't going to move by myself. Then I started to wonder if anyone did see me. "I mean really, I'm hurting here," I thought to myself. "I can't get up by myself. I need someone's assistance." Sooner or later they came. I was upset that I wouldn't be able to run the same anymore. Jackrabbit wouldn't move the way he used to. Yeah it sucked.

I had the same feeling after I was attacked. I kept thinking, "Can my body take this pain? Will I be able to get up? I know God hears and sees me lying here, will He come immediately to my rescue?"

If you have ever been injured before, you understand that it takes a lot to recover from being hurt. It feels like starting all over again after you heal and have to condition yourself back into shape. After I was attacked, my body had to go through so many difficult changes and I felt like I wasn't ready for them. But deep down inside I wasn't going to let anything stop me from moving forward in my life. I had to remember what it felt like to be on the track again and think back to the times I've worked hard to accomplish my goals. I've been there before, I told myself. I knew what it took to get in shape. So I did it.

I realized that anything you must accomplish in life is possible if you get up and put a plan together. It's a mindset. Go to work and maintain your efforts throughout the process. It's time for you to run and see what the end is going to be like. There will be some hurdles in life, but don't give up, even if you fall.

CHAPTER FIVE

"DID THIS REALLY HAPPEN?"

> "Violence is the use of physical force, usually with intent to violate or destroy. Violence is a violation of God's perfect order." ~Herbert Lockyer, Sr.

When I was alone after my attack, I was on my knees with my head bowed and my eyes closed saying, "Lord I'm waiting on you to come rescue me. Where are you, God? What in the world just happened to me? Did this really just happen to me?" I couldn't believe what was going on. While it was happening, all I knew to do was pray to God. My exact words were, "God you know where I am right now and I need you to save me. Help me Lord. I don't know what is going to happen to me, but I need you so bad right now."

So many things continued to run through my mind at that time. Have you ever needed God so bad for something and wondered if He was going to show up on time?

Our time is not God's time though. I had to figure that out during my captivity. I wondered if it was all a dream or was I hallucinating?

> Have you ever been caught off guard by an unusual situation? What happened to you? Did it scare you or cause you to feel confused? Did you wonder if it really happened to you? What did you do about it?

No, this is really happening to me I reminded myself. I wanted to yell my prayers to God, but instead, I decided to keep them inside my mind, the only place that felt safe at the time. Those prayers kept me calm and sane, and there was literally nothing else I could do while hoping that God would get me out of that situation. I've never been tortured so much in my life. I thought my time on earth was coming to an end. I thought, "I'm not going to make it out of here." But something kept pulling on me to stay conscious and pray to God my Father and that's what I did. I prayed long and hard, even while I was getting beat down.

At some point during the robbery, my attacker took the handcuffs off me and left me alone. I heard a door slam but a voice within me said, "Don't get up yet, don't get up." A few moments later it said, "Ok get up." I slowly got up from the floor and I could feel the blood dripping down my face.

"Aaaaaah!" My back was hurting and I was wobbling, weak from the excruciating pain. I was very aware of my internal being because I knew what had just happened so I walked slowly and carefully into the other room. I was hoping that I wouldn't get caught by surprise again. When I went into the other room, my coworker's pants were down, and the contents of her wallet were all over the place. She looked stunned from what just happened and I asked her if she was alright. She mumbled a reply and I said, "I'm going outside to see if they are gone so we can get help. We gotta get out of here."

I started running to get help, and I jumped over the fence and everything even though I was hurt, bleeding, and my stomach was messed up. I guess my adrenaline was just pushing me to keep going.

I was crossing the street to knock on someone's door for help when I saw my coworker get in her car and start it up. I went and jumped in the car with her, saying, "What in the world just happened? We need to go to the police," but she said, "I don't know what to do, I gotta get out of here, he has all my information, I gotta move. My identity has been stolen, this person knows who I am." She said she didn't want to go to the police station, and I was like, "What do you mean? The police station is the safest place to be right now!"

I couldn't argue with a brick wall so I just said, "Take me home." I didn't have my keys or my phone and I didn't want to knock on anybody's door for help in my neighborhood because I didn't want them to be in my business. I walked about 15-20 minutes to the nearest store, praying the whole way. "God You kept me; You got me out of this situation, thank You God." All I could do was cry and thank God that I was still alive. I couldn't believe what had just happened to me.

Even though I was still in pain, my goal was to get to a safe place. I basically walked through my pain and with each step I thought about Jesus being beaten, brutalized, and crucified. I couldn't compare my situation to what He went through but I referenced it and I knew that the blood of Jesus covered me and He kept me. It kept me moving toward my destination of safety.

I made it to a pizzeria and went in very reserved and low-key, not wanting to draw attention to myself. With blood on my head, face, and clothing, I quietly asked the restaurant owner if I could use their phone to call 911, saying I had just been in a situation and didn't feel too well. They quickly allowed me to use the phone. As I was waiting I was very aware of the pain I was in and it even hurt at times to breathe. The police arrived and began to question me about what happened. They sent other officers to check out my story and they found my coworker's house and saw that everything was the way that I had described.

The ambulance came to transport me to the hospital. As I was riding in the ambulance, I could feel the EMT pressing down on my stomach, wondering why it was so big. They injected me with something to help me calm down and deal with the pain. After we arrived at the hospital I knew that a long night was ahead of me. I was just looking into the sky wondering what would happen next. "Lord what just happened to me?"

I found out that I needed surgery immediately and actually had multiple surgeries for about six-eight hours, including a colostomy, which means that part of my colon was brought through my abdomen, where an opening was made. I had an ostomy bag attached to the end of my colon to drain waste so that the other parts of my colon could heal. [1] I was in the hospital for about two and a half weeks.

When I woke up from my surgery, I still couldn't believe what just happened to me and all the things the doctors did just to put me back together. I didn't want to be here, but I had to stay in order to recover and heal. This was all new to me and I had to adjust.

I could have been in the hospital longer but I asked the doctor, "Do you believe in prayer?" To every nurse and anyone else who came into my hospital room, I asked them, "Do you believe in prayer?" If they said yes, I asked them to pray for me. A nurse prayed for me every night.

I said to the doctor, "I don't belong in here. How do I get out of here?" He said I had to push through and walk laps around the hallways. "The more you walk, the faster you can get out."

The doctor wrote everything on the white board in my room from A to Z, exactly what I needed to do to get out of there. If he told me to walk a lap I would do two laps in order to get my strength back. It was a struggle at times to get up and out of the bed. I definitely wasn't complaining, but I had to get used to it all. I was in pain but I got through it all with the support of my family.

CHAPTER SIX

THE SUPPORT OF FAMILY

"It's impossible to get through a tough situation by yourself. Who do you call on when you need help?" ~Marcel Anderson

When the ambulance first brought me to the hospital, there was a doctor and an investigator asking me questions immediately. I didn't have any contact information or identification on me. I was trembling, shaking, and cold. I tried to think of who I could call. I finally called my mother and it was really late. I actually had to keep calling, she may have been asleep. When my mom picked up I said, "Mom, I just want to let you know, I have been involved in a robbery." She said, "Boy stop playing, no you haven't," and didn't believe it. I ended up putting her on the phone with the doctor after I told her, "I need to go into surgery right now."

To hear my family tell it, as soon as my brother Aaron heard that I had been attacked, he got up immediately, started putting on clothes, and got the cousins on the phone line because he was angry and upset, like, "Who did this to my brother? We gotta find them and get up there to make sure that we protect him."

When I woke up from surgery, and opened my eyes, everything was a blur, but I was aware that my college friends Randy, Alvin, and Brent were there first (my brother had contacted them). My parents, brothers, cousins, extended family, and other friends began to arrive by that night from South Carolina, as well as my principal and teachers from the school where I worked at the time.

Many people came to the hospital wanting to see me and find out what had happened. As other people began hearing what had happened to me and all of the surgeries I had gone through, they starting thinking the worst. Some of them thought that I was going to die. They were coming in crying and leaving crying; they were praying that my healing would be fast. People constantly came over the course of the two and a half weeks that I was in the hospital.

My family was curious about what took place and they wanted answers. They wanted to know as much as possible about the situation and who was involved, where they were, and how did that person respond to the situation. They wanted to make sure I would be protected once I left the hospital. As long as I was in the hospital, I had an alias name and hospital police protection.

The family was constantly asking questions and as I told them the story you could hear the rage in their voices and see it in their faces. They were very upset, very frustrated, very mad, and very angry – they wanted to respond in an abnormal manner, however, in my constant conversation with them, I said, "Vengeance is the Lord's to repay." I said, "Let's just continue to pray and I will be fine."

For the duration of my recovery my family was trying to solve the case of my attack. I kept saying God was going to handle it but I knew they were not listening and still trying to solve the case.

Throughout the process my family was there with me. They helped me walk around the hospital, they took turns visiting with me, they would go home to South Carolina and then come all the way back to North Carolina. All six of my brothers and sisters came and stayed overnight. They spent a lot of money to travel back and forth to see me. My mother stayed in North Carolina for over a month when it happened because I couldn't take care of myself at first when I got out of the hospital; I needed a lot of help.

In the midst of all that I was trained in how to change my ostomy bag. Wow! Living with an ostomy bag was completely new and different for me. I struggled many times trying to change it and had no idea what I was doing. Thank God for friends who were nurses. The simple fact that my mother practiced nursing helped so much. She knew exactly what to do when I needed her the most– I was not only her son, but also her patient. I could remember my twin brother Marcus traveling back and forth to handle my paperwork with the school system - my insurance, paychecks, etc. My family communicated with my church and the church donated funds, supplied food, cards, balloons, flowers, prayer, and encouragement. They prayed with me and for me, fussed over me and showed major concern.

People continued to visit me from all over Virginia, the Carolinas, Atlanta, and beyond. At least three people got speeding tickets because they were trying to get to me so fast. My fraternity brothers of Kappa Alpha Psi constantly came and called and showed support with cards and money. My own chapter from South Carolina constantly checked on me and offered their support. The hospital staff said they never saw so many people come in and out during the course of someone's hospital stay.

The support of your family is so important when you go through something like this. Even if you don't have a big family, prayerfully there is someone you can trust to support you in your situation. I don't know what I would have done if my family, friends, and church family weren't there. I thank God for them. They were the best support system I could have during that time of my life.

Name your support system. Think about the people you counted on when you went through something tough in your life. Why were they so important in your personal process? Could you have made it without them?

_____

_____

_____

_____

_____

_____

Once I was out of the hospital I didn't immediately go home. I had a friend who worked in a hotel and gave us a good discount for two weeks so I went and stayed there at first, which I think was good for my protection as well as for the convenience of having my room and bedding cleaned and things like that. Even there I constantly had visitors. I was able to walk the halls in the hotel just like I did at the hospital, which was necessary for me to get better. My close friend Amy at the time came and stayed with my mother and assisted her with anything she needed. Amy actually drove us wherever we needed to go and helped throughout the entire process. Amy was such a big help. I don't know if I could have made it through some nights without her conversation or presence. There is nothing a like special person in your life who cares so much about you. As I was dealing with all the changes in my body, help was so much needed.

Over time, I had to go get more bags for my colostomy. I was still learning how to clean the bags myself and sometimes the stuff would just come out, but I got good at it to the point where my friends would come over and be like, "Hey man, what are you doing?" and I would be like, "Oh, I'm just cleaning my ostomy bag, just chilling." Sometimes they would be like, "Hey man, what's that smell? You need to change your bag!"

One day my friends decided to do something nice, so they came over and cooked spaghetti. I wasn't really supposed to eat that because my system still wasn't ready. I had a little of it with some salad and next thing I know, my bag got filled all of a sudden and it was overrunning. It was nasty, I didn't know what to do but my mom helped; I actually had to change the bag like three or four times within the hour.

I had friends and family members including my niece who went to school for nursing and they volunteered to help me change my bag. My situation actually inspired my sister Ursula to pursue nursing because she enjoyed helping with my care and watching what the nurses did. She is actually a registered nurse now.

After I moved back home, I bought a car. I didn't have one before and my family was concerned about me walking everywhere. I was also getting used to living with my ostomy bag so I didn't drive all the time, but I was able to drive when I needed to. I had not been working for about 6 months and the doctor wouldn't release me to go back to work, so there was a concern of how to pay for the car. My coworkers in the school system kept donating their leave (vacation time) to me so that I would have a full paycheck while I was out. If I didn't have that, I don't know how I would have been supported outside of my family and they had already sacrificed so much. It was a journey thinking about work and how things were going to get paid. I struggled at times, but God made a way. It was a process and I'm thankful that the process allowed me to see how important my family was to me.

As the days and weeks went on, my family constantly asked about the case and were concerned about my safety. I moved into a new place and had a lot of help from my family and frat brothers. My family came back up from South Carolina and we had a big dinner cooked by my brother Aaron. We played games and made great memories in the middle of a challenging situation. I started calling everybody and telling them to come over and celebrate. There is nothing like celebrating life with your family after experiencing something so detrimental.

When was the last time you celebrated life with your family? List three different gatherings you and your family had in the last year.

_____

_____

_____

CHAPTER SEVEN

MENTAL RECOVERY

> "A grown man with a childlike mentality won't make it far. In order to change, change your situation, change your environment, your friends, your actions, but first you have to change your mind..." ~ Dr. Aaron T. Anderson (Mr. Table Talk)

I was out of work for about six months but my principal held my job until I was able to return. I had to have another surgery about five months after the first one to reverse the colostomy – which doesn't always happen. Because I was an athlete and had always kept my body in great shape I was able to withstand and recover and was only in the hospital for about three to four days after the second surgery.

Through that process, I was by myself, just me and the Lord, and I sometimes contemplated, "I'm about to get somebody," but I never entertained that voice or those who spoke those words to me on a regular basis. I received constant calls from people asking, "Do you want us to handle this for you?" in regards to retribution, but I didn't take them up on their offer.

About three months after the incident happened, I started getting professional psychiatric counseling for about one and a half years as well as spiritual counseling from my pastor. At first I didn't want to go. When I was in the hospital, a counselor, chaplain, and crisis intervention program representatives came to see me and I would smile and politely say, "Thank you so much, God bless you, I appreciate you. I'm fine. Thank you so much for coming in, you guys have a blessed day." But inside I said, "I'm a man, I don't need no counselor." I did end up going and it helped a lot, especially the professional counseling.

In there I was able to vent, I was able to yell, I was able to cry, I was able to scream, I was able to say how I felt. I was tense and I was still worried. I had to relocate; my whole system had to change in order to accommodate what happened. From day to day, I wasn't sure about what would happen.

In addition to that let me tell you how good God is. When the situation happened, I did not yet have benefits at my job. The paperwork had just been processed and my benefits were scheduled to go into effect on February 1st but the incident occurred on January 1st. However, because of what happened, my case went to the crisis intervention program and they reached out to me and my parents to help us with the situation financially. I could show you my bills right now - they amounted to almost $100,000 and I paid nothing. The only thing I paid was the co-pay for medicine and things of that nature. Literally almost $100,000 worth of surgeries, medicines, and tests were all paid for.

What I learned from listening to and working with the crisis intervention support group, showed me that there are resources within the community that can help you with a situation like mine. At that moment you may not realize how important they are for your life, but you can benefit from them tremendously; I know I have.

If something like this ever happened or happens to you, don't be afraid to search for support and help from outside resources. Of course I feared at times what others would say to me when I walked into their office as a male victim, but over time I grew to understand that I could not lose my true identity.

"Before I formed you in the womb I knew you, and before you were born I consecrated you; I appointed you a prophet to the nations." Jeremiah 1:5

Don't Lose your True Identity

"Who are you and what are you called to do?" These are questions I constantly ask myself on a daily basis. After experiencing something so devastating, I have to remind myself of who I am in God and what I'm called to do in Him. I realize and understand that God created me in His own image and I'm created to stay strong, even when I can't put my mind around it. Daily I have to allow God to transform my mind in order for me to move where He wants me to go. I can't lose my true identity no matter what happens to me in life. No matter what people say or don't say about me, I must stay true to myself and the person God has designed me to be. Even when you feel like you want to give up on yourself, you have to reach deeper within your soul and remind yourself why you are here on earth.

When I went back to work, my family didn't want me to go back and be in that environment with the other person, not knowing if she had any involvement in what happened to me. I can't say that she did or not, I just had to wait and see.

The investigator in my case said that her non-responsiveness was a typical reaction from a victim; that when they are in shock, they don't want anything to do with the other person involved, etc. However, it still concerns me that she never personally expressed anything to me at all during this entire process. I was attacked while I was helping her, and I don't understand why she had no concern for my safety. Why didn't she inquire about my condition while I was in the hospital? I have never accused her of anything, it is just a major concern to me – in my personal evaluation of her behavior and responses, and it makes me think differently about her than before.

She and I both ended our employment at the school the same year. That summer, I didn't want to work. To be honest, it took everything in me to even go back to work, especially as a teacher working in special education with students who have complex emotional needs and challenges. I was going through my own physical, emotional, and psychological challenges. I made it through and then did everything in my power not to work that summer. I ended up having a part time job to help me get through but it was not really enough. It was a mental journey. I thought about how I was going to get through the summer financially since I was only working a part time job had no events scheduled that would bring in extra income.

I got so late on my car notes and insurance payments. I actually went six or seven months not paying - I didn't have the money so there was nothing I could really do. Eventually I turned the car in. That is when my walking journey began– for about a year and a half until I was in the position to get a new car.

It wasn't that easy walking from work and riding the bus, but that was my only means of transportation. I knew I had to do something and I constantly worked a little extra and saved towards another car. Every time I started saving it seemed like something came up. Have you ever felt like that before? You get to an almost good place in your life and BAM - the walls come tumbling down again. Daily my constant focus was to stay invested. I had to invest in myself so I wouldn't lose my sense of direction for my life even though things weren't always going my way.

I had to keep my mind focused on the things that were above in heaven and not beneath. As easy as it sounds, it wasn't always that easy, but I kept my mind transformed and renewed in the Word of God. God's Word was food for my thought processing.

How often do you read God's word? Where do you read God's word when you are frustrated with a tough situation in your Life?

_____

_____

_____

What are some things that help you get through a mentally challenging situation?

List 3 of them below.

1. _____

2. _____

3. _____

CHAPTER EIGHT

DO YOU BELIEVE IN PRAYER?

> "I'm trying to regain the spiritual energy to stay focused." ~Marcel Anderson

There have been many days and nights that I needed something to get me through my traumatic situation and I can truly say prayer has given me many answers. I don't know if you believe in God or if you believe in the power of prayer but let me tell you that prayer works and it changes things. When no one else is there to help you during that most disturbing moment in your life, God and prayer will see you through it. It's not hard to pray. When I can't find the words to say, I refer back to The Lord's Prayer:

The Lord's Prayer

"This, then, is how you should pray: "'Our Father in heaven, hallowed be your name, your kingdom come, your will be done, on earth as it is in heaven.

Give us today our daily bread. And forgive us our debts, as we also have forgiven our debtors. And lead us not into temptation, but deliver us from the evil one.

For if you forgive other people when they sin against you, your heavenly Father will also forgive you. But if you do not forgive others their sins, your Father will not forgive your sins." Matthew 6: 9-15

How often do you pray?

I pray_____ a day.

I pray _____ a week.

Prayer has power over everything. Our God has and can act intelligently in any part of His creation. Although some people think prayer is a waste of time, I charge you today to do more of it. The Bible declares, "The effective, fervent prayer of a righteous man avails much" (James 5: 16). This means that your prayer can and will be answered when you submit to God and trust in Him with your whole heart. It's the prayer course you must get on and stay on. Stay in the lane of faith knowing that God is helping you. When you pray with the right heart and spirit unto God, you start to see the right result. I saw God moving constantly on my behalf when I prayed to Him daily – and I mean daily. All I could think of is that old Baptist song, "I know that prayer will, prayer will, prayer will OH, change things."

Prayer will change things. Just tell yourself, "I do believe in it." Once you believe in it, your confidence in God begins to build more than before. It's a daily walk. My confidence in God started to build daily as I took one day at a time. I knew God would grant me the desires of my heart, because His Word said so. I had no other choice but to lean on Him and my confidence started to build because of Him.

"Now this is the confidence that we have in Him, that if we ask anything according to His will, he hears us. And if we know that He hears us, whatever we ask, we know that we have the petitions that we have asked of Him." 1 John 5:14

Spiritual Recovery

During my prayer time I gained confidence in God daily to get me through my situation mentally, spiritually, and physically, and He did just that. I'm a living witness to it today.

In addition to prayer I just began to soak in the Word of God. I re-enrolled in seminary school because I felt like I needed a spiritual hospital to get me back on track. That semester allowed me to hear God's voice again. This really saved me because I was surrounded by other people who were in the Word of God, having constant conversations about the Word of God. It was a safe haven for me – going to chapel service, being with likeminded people, it all built me back up. God challenged me and tested me concerning what I was going to do with my gift. I said I wasn't going to sit on it; I exercised it, conditioned it, and worked it out. I said, "Lord, I'm going to grow closer to you versus drift away from you." I don't know what or who you are connected to, but after experiencing something so challenging in your life, it is so important to connect to something greater than yourself.

The Holy Spirit

"And I will pray the Father, and he shall give you another Comforter, that he may abide with you forever." John 14:16

When I regained understanding that the Holy Spirit was my Comforter, I allowed myself to connect with Him daily. The Holy Spirit led me to do and say the right things, even when I wanted to say something differently. Sometimes it's better to think before you speak. I know, because it helps me get through some challenging moments at times. The Holy Spirit was my guide in moving forward with my life. He was the driver and constantly directed my thoughts down the right spiritual road. Going on that mental journey by yourself will have you off on the side of the road. It's not good to do this process by yourself, even if you feel like you are man or woman enough. The right help is always needed and the Holy Spirit helped me to pray and gave me the courage to stay in a good place throughout my movement. I needed something other than myself to find that next place of stability.

In order to keep myself stable, I started working part-time at JC Penney and I knew I needed to get a full time job but I also needed to be in school. My family was still supportive of me while reminding me that I needed to work full-time. I think I also felt I needed to be away from the school system because of its association with what happened. I took a year off but finally went back because I needed to support myself and also due to my love of working with youth. Daily as I worked in the school system I realized the importance of inspiring young people to become more than the way they saw themselves.

I especially wanted to bring awareness and make a difference in the lives of all young men. This began happening once I shared my story. One young man told me that he had been molested since the age of three. His cousins would pass him around and take advantage of him. During that time, he didn't fully understand what was happening to him and he never spoke about it until after he heard me tell my story. He had never told any-one prior to telling me, not even his mother.

In situations where you have been hurt, violated, and abused, you can temporarily lose your voice. Through my process of spiritual recovery, God allowed me to re-discover my voice. My relationship with God caused me to tune in to His "channel," where I could hear His voice and see how He was molding me back into who He de-signed me to be. He had already placed the words in my mouth, now it was time for me to turn up the volume.

CHAPTER NINE

SPEAK UP

Why it Matters

> "Men, as well as women, are victimized by violence. Sexual abuse and rape create substantial physical and psychological harm to male victims and perpetuate the cycle of violence. Men and boys are less likely to report the violence and seek services due to the following challenges: the stigma of being a male victim, the perceived failure to conform to the macho stereotype, the fear of not being believed, the denial of victim status, and the lack of support from society, family members, and friends." [2]

"Speak up for those who cannot speak for themselves; ensure justice for those being crushed." Proverbs 3:18

Did you know that the statistics for male victims of sexual assault and violence are real? Women are not the only ones who experience these types of violent attacks on their life. Have you ever done research on male victims of abuse? I didn't until I became a victim myself.

Boy, was that something for me to express out loud. I tried everything to hold it back, but I said it and now it's out. I'm speaking up about what happened to me and turning up my volume because this affects men all over the world as well. There is something to learn and understand about abuse. Every situation isn't the same, however they all produce similar effects.

I'm a man, and normally men don't communicate about these types of situations with others because of shame, guilt, and how they think others will perceive them. In this case, I'm taking the initiative to tell other men who may share the same story if not worse.

When I started researching and learning more about men who were victims of sexual assault, I wouldn't have believed the numbers except for the fact that I was included in those numbers. Oh yeah, I was reading about myself during the discovery of male sexual assault victims. To be honest it was somewhat hard for me to grasp and understand that I was among these staggering statistics and one day I would speak up about what happened to me. That was a struggle and challenge at the time, but I made it through by the grace of God. It was hard to talk about it. It has been a fight and a battle with

God, others, and myself, even in still thinking about that abuser who wanted to shut me up. I was faced with death. He invaded my space and wanted me to say nothing.

I just knew I was going to take my last breath when that happened, but thank God I'm alive to speak about my process. I'm still living. Even now as I tell you about my story, it's not always easy, but I know that it is only right to speak up and share the truth with other men and women who are victims of violence and abuse to tell them, "you are not alone in your situation." If this has been your experience, my prayer is that you would understand that there's someone else in the world waiting for your voice to be heard, for you to speak up and share the truth.

Yes I'm talking to you, the one who cries at night and keeps silent because you felt bad or sad about not being accepted by others. You remember the days and nights when it was just you and God, and no one was around to hear you or help you get through those real moments.

Those moments caused you pain and heartache, but deep down inside, something kept you moving. Even now you have asked yourself, "How did I make it and who is keeping me through this?" Speaking up means speaking to God about all of your troubles and worries. Speaking up means that you have to open your heart for forgiveness and not resent the fact that something was taken away from you. Now you can move on and speak to others about your situation.

I say this because I know that God cares about more than just me. God cares for His children, even if something bad happens to them. The moments I've spent with God about this situation have caused me to reevaluate myself and think twice about who I am and what I'm called to do on earth. In the midst of my loneliness, I really went through a withdrawal stage where I didn't want to be bothered with anyone and it came to the point where I didn't even want to speak to myself about it, even though I knew God was standing right beside me. I call that phase, "Going through it."

You are Not Alone:

- According to the National Coalition against Domestic Violence, 16% of adult men who reported being raped and/or physically assaulted were assaulted by a current or former spouse, cohabitating partner, boyfriend/girlfriend, or date.
- According to the National Center for Victims of Crime, men experience many of the same psychological reactions to violence as women.
- 40% of gay and bisexual men will experience abuse at the hands of an intimate partner.

• In the National Violence against Women Survey, approximately 23% of men reported being raped, physically assaulted, and/or stalked by a male intimate partner. 7% of men reported such violence by a wife or female cohabitant.

• According to a Bureau of Justice Statistics 2004 report, 5.5% of male homicide victims were murdered by a spouse, ex-spouse, boyfriend or girlfriend.

• Women committing lethal acts of violence against their male partners are 7-10 times more likely than men to have acted in self-defense. [2]

Good will Come of This

The Old Testament gives us a great example in the story of Joseph, who went through terrible suffering, being sold into slavery by his brothers, unfairly accused of a crime and falsely imprisoned. Finally, after a dozen years, he was put in a role of great authority where he could save the lives of his family and many others. This is what he said to his brothers in Genesis 50:20: "You intended to harm me, but God intended it for good to accomplish what is now being done, the saving of many lives."

If you're committed to God, He promises that He can and will take whatever pain you're experiencing and draw something good from it. You might say, "No, He can't in my circumstance. The harm was too great, the damage was too extreme, and the depth of my suffering has been too much. No, in my case there's no way God can cause any good to emerge."

Jesus said in John 16:33, "I have told you these things so that in me you may have peace. You will have suffering in this world. But be courageous! I have conquered the world." In other words, He offers us the two very things we need when we're hurting: peace to deal with our present and courage to deal with our future. How? Because He has conquered the world! Through His own suffering and death, He has deprived this world of its ultimate power over you. Suffering doesn't have the last word anymore. Death doesn't have the last word anymore. God has the last word!

Hard to Tell

At first when I thought about my assault, I felt a little nervous about sharing it with the public. This was all new and fresh to me. "This is going to be different," I told myself. Well, I am a man and telling someone about what I've been through, was just not something I felt strongly about expressing. Normally that's what's planted in the mind of men around the world, that if something so detrimental happened to you, you normally don't speak up about it. Men's pride issues get in the way.

Pride can hurt and kill a man when it prevents him from coming forth and speaking up on anything, not just abuse. As men, we sometimes have the tendency to hold on to things and not let things go. We can work so hard to provide for our families yet lack emotional connections with them.

I witness pride being an issue in my own family. Watching my father work daily and provide for our family, it was rare that he showed any true emotions. However, men must show some type of emotions because we are human. The misrepresentation of men and emotions is that men don't cry or don't talk about "sensitive" issues in most cases. That seemed to be the case with my father. I love him and thank God for his drive in working, but does he really have an understanding of how to speak up and express his true feelings towards his family? It's not that he doesn't care about us, being expressive is just not something that my father saw his father do when he was growing up as a little boy.

For most men, we see our fathers operate in a proud way and never get the opportunity to release our true emotions. Yes! Our emotions can also keep us from not speaking up, because as men we think we are so hard, but we can be softer than a pillow when a brick falls on our foot. We allow ourselves to become distant and emotionless when holding our true feelings inside.

I didn't want to do that with my situation. I knew I had to share my emotions in order to get past it, even with the wrong spirit standing over my shoulder, telling me, "Why speak up? No one is going to listen and you're better off by yourself in a closet crying yourself to sleep."

The fact is, your mind can play tricks on you and it's important that you speak up to God and let Him know how you feel. It's ok to speak up and let God know what's on your heart and mind. He is a loving God who cares and knows what you are going through.

Sometimes during a situation like this, the 'worthless spirit' can tell you that you are not worth moving forward in your God-given gift. Even the thought of what others may say about you can hinder you from speaking up. These are just a few things that I experienced before moving forward and taking the initiative and courage to speak up about what happened to me. Honestly, I never thought something like this would ever happen to me.

It took some time for me to grab hold of reality, understanding and believing that I was still alive and would be asked by so many people about the details of what happened to me. To be honest, I got tired of the questions, but I never showed it to anyone. What happened to me was always on my mind. It lived with me. It became me and I had to learn how to adjust to another way of living. I was still living but living with something else attached to my name. That was not a bad thing, but it was a change that I had to get used to. I had to position myself for the better and not the worse. It was so important for me to develop the prayer life that I spoke about in the previous chapter. Prayer changes things and it changed me to the fifth power. I'm still living because of it.

What Will Happen if I Tell?

I kept thinking about all of the negative things that could happen to me if I told someone about my incident. My life could be in jeopardy. Well, my life was in jeopardy. My family's life could be in jeopardy. A lot of things could take place if I spoke up boldly about what I experienced. The attacker's voice kept popping back up in my head and his sound was very clear in my mind on a daily basis. It was that voice playing tricks on me, the devil, the enemy, who knows? It was an aggravating voice that had to go.

I knew I had to do something in order to move forward, so I never entertained that voice. Yes it was difficult at times to ignore, but as I started speaking and encouraging myself, I knew I could build my temple (mind, body, and soul). "This is not going to hold me down," I said. I never let that voice get in the way of God's voice. Prayer, singing, prayer, laughing, prayer, and talking to God gave me more confidence to release that voice from my mind.

The mind is powerful and it's a playground where thoughts can linger and cause you to act or say the wrong thing. I had to be mindful of all of that when I thought about speaking up. The more I conditioned my mind with God's word, the more it became very real that I was going to make it. I had to take time to study to show myself approved, so I wouldn't be ashamed of the truth (Timothy 2:5).

Yeah, that's God's Word, but it's also the truth of what happened to me. The thoughts of the attacker popped back into my mind very clearly every day. His threatening words that he would come after me if I said anything were real and not something to play with. I was even nervous and timid at times, but I felt confident enough in God to know He was going to keep me safe.

It was a test of my faith and a witness of what I was living that would actually help others and then me. I started to realize and recognize that this wasn't about me, but about saving lives. I spoke up and here I am.

Speaking up is a Must

I spoke up because I knew I couldn't live without helping someone else through the same situation. After talking to so many people about my situation, many of them started to open up to me in different settings I was in. I had students during the school day talk about how they were molested as a child. Because I spoke up, they felt confident enough to tell me their story and I was often the first person they ever told.

Deep down inside my heart, I knew God was pulling on me to share my story but not to this magnitude. I knew it would help someone, but I never thought that so many people experienced some type of violence or abuse in their life. After singing and speaking at different events, the emails and sometimes phone calls came through from both females and males who were expressing their story with me for the first time. How do I react to those stories? What do I say to them? What is my purpose in their lives? I constantly ask God to give me the right words to say to them and He does. Many of those individuals have now opened up to other people in their families and allowed their voice to be heard. I told them to always "trust in the Lord with all of their hearts and lean not unto their own understanding and he would direct their path" (Proverbs 3:5).

At times it was kind of hard for them to release their story but over time they too found the right courage inside their heart to release their story and not allow that inner voice to keep them from telling a secret at the right time. It's so important to consult with a specialist or spiritual counselor as you transition into confidence with your story. It was because I sought out professional counseling and visited my pastor or confided in the right people in my family that I was able to become secure in telling my story.

I don't know who that specialist could be in your life, but find them and allow them to lead you down the right path. I also encourage you to try Jesus, because I found Him to be more than all right with me. He saved me and allows me to learn how to use the right language in the right settings. It's so important that you get the proper guidance and help as you move to the place of release. It will ease the process. Releasing yourself is good. Don't hold it to yourself, but connect with the right person as you plan to speak up.

The Outcome May Surprise You

As I shared, I was surprised that many people saw me as an outlet to plug into. They opened up their secrets to me. I was someone they felt like they could trust. They felt some type of connection with me even though their situations were different from mine. The outcome of the individuals telling their stories caused me to understand and realize that I wasn't by myself. I don't have to worry about being alone in this situation.

You have to understand that, even if someone invaded your three feet of space, God is with you. I realize that "greater is He that is in me than He that is in the world" (1 John 4:4). I've learned over time, God has predestined all of us for something greater than we can even imagine.

Together we must keep our heads up, no matter our situations. Even if you are not a victim of abuse or violence, there could be another situation blocking you from reaching your destination. I don't know what that is, but I will encourage you to move past it. Speak to it and never allow it to overtake you. Today is the day we all speak up and channel our energy into the things that are positive in this life.

Push Through the Hard Days

Life is going to bring its challenges and we may not always understand them all. But I do know that we are all born with special gifts and talents that will help someone else recognize their gifts and talents also. I still have to take it one day at a time, but in my daily movements, I'm making sure my mind, body, and soul are being taken care of. I'm working on me daily. I'm reflecting on me so when I'm challenged by a rough situation, it won't cause me to stray from what I'm designed to do for that day.

My daily motivation is life itself. I'm thankful to be alive. I'm motivated by God, His Son Jesus and the musical gifts that are planted on the inside of me. I have to remind myself that something great is going to happen in my life. In the midst of discomfort, I remind myself I'm still living for a reason and when I speak on what I've been through, others can be blessed by what I say. I speak up today because I'm still here.

Today, I encourage anyone who has a story to speak up and talk to the right person about your situation. It will help someone else and it will help you get through life so much easier. The time is now that you grab hold to what belongs to you and reach past your situation. You were born a winner; never let anyone tell you any differently about what you can and can't do. Speak the truths of life and it will set you free. (John 8: 32).

Self-Check

When I started doing research on male victims of violence, I learned that there were different types of abuse and I want to share them with you.

Types of abuse:

- Physical abuse is the use of physical force against another in a way that injures that person or puts the victim at risk of being injured. Physical abuse ranges from physical restraint to murder and may include pushing, throwing, tripping, slapping, hitting, kicking, punching, grabbing, choking, shaking, etc.

- Emotional/Psychological abuse is any use of words, tone, action, or lack of action meant to control, hurt or demean another person. Emotional abuse typically includes ridicule, intimidation, or coercion. Verbal abuse is included in this category.

- Sexual abuse is any forced or coerced sexual act or behavior motivated to acquire power and control over another person. It includes forced sexual contact and contact that demeans, humiliates or instigates feelings of shame or vulnerability, particularly in regards to the body, sexual performance or sexuality.

- Financial abuse is the use or misuse of the financial or monetary resources of the partner or of the partnership without the partner's freely given consent. It can include preventing the partner from working or jeopardizing his/her employment so as to prevent them from gaining financial independence.

- Identity abuse is using personal characteristics to demean, manipulate and control another person.

- Spiritual abuse is using the victim's religious or spiritual beliefs to manipulate them. It can include preventing the victim from practicing their beliefs or ridiculing his/her beliefs. [3]

Have you ever been subject to any of these kinds of abuse but never spoke up about it? Start today by writing it out and work with God to build the confidence you need and want. Connect with someone you can trust. Your story matters.   Turn up the volume.

Speak up and tell your own Story:

_____

_____

_____

_____

_____

_____

_____

_____

_____

_____

_____

_____

_____

_____

_____

_____

_____

_____

_____

_____

_____

_____

CHAPTER TEN

REGAINING TRUST

Have you ever let someone borrow some money from you and they never gave it back? Did you let them borrow some money a second time? What was the next outcome? Has one of your friends ever told you that they would pick you up for work but never showed up? Did you ever ask them for another ride again? If you were ever stranded again, did you think to call that friend who never picked you up the first time? If no, why? Probably because you couldn't trust them.

> *"It is better to trust in the LORD than to put confidence in man." Psalms 118:8*

> "Trust God first and you will gain the confidence you need in order to understand how to reconnect to society." ~ Marcel Anderson

Trusting someone or a group of individuals after a terrible encounter with them can sometimes be hard. For me, I had a hard time trusting other people after my incident. I would constantly stay isolated from people when I was asked to go to different outings. In this case it wasn't the fact that they did anything wrong, I just couldn't really trust people because of what happened to me.

I especially had a hard time trusting women even though I enjoy spending time with women who have their head on straight. In this case, my internal feelings caused me to be distanced from society and caused my mind to be alert when dealing with myself and other people. However, over time, I continue to work on my trust issues. It was difficult at times; I had to learn how to ease up just a little, but still be cautious. I truly think it is part of the entire experience that I encountered.

Mainly because I started putting the majority of my trust in God, things started to get better for me in that area. I constantly reminded myself that Proverbs 3:5 says to, "Trust in the Lord with all of your heart and lean not unto your own understanding and in all thy ways acknowledge him and He will direct your path." That is what happens when you trust God; you can begin to trust others. I constantly put all of my trust in God and allowed Him to lead me down that path of trusting others and then myself again. Thank you Lord. Even though someone has done something bad to you or even caused much harm in your life, don't allow that to affect you to the point that you isolate yourself from society. Hold on to God's unchanging hand and everything will work out fine.

Love in Spite Of

God loves you and it is important that we love others "in spite of." Sometimes I didn't know how to respond or express how I felt towards myself and other people in my circle. My feelings were not just hurt; I became calloused and felt nothing towards them in my heart. I constantly became challenged by how much I couldn't understand what happened to me and who did it. In my case, I don't know the person who did this to me. My case is still pending.

I have wondered daily who could have done something like this to me and yet how am I supposed to love them "in spite of." I really needed the Lord's help on this one. We can't understand how to love anyone else without first learning how to love God and then ourselves by getting acquainted with God and His thoughts toward us through His Word. After going through that process we can see that God gave up something for us so that we could experience love. Why can't we do the same for someone else by loving them in spite of what they have done? Loving others reconnects us to our first love which is God.

Forgiveness will set you Free?

By casting my cares upon the Lord, my life involved daily conditioning and exercising of my mind, body, and soul. I kept working out my spirit to find true understanding on the importance of forgiveness. Generally, forgiveness is a decision to let go of resentment and thoughts of revenge. The act that hurt or offended you might always remain a part of your life, but forgiveness can lessen its grip on you and help you focus on other positive parts of your life. Forgiveness can even lead to feelings of understanding, empathy, and compassion for the one who hurt you.

Forgiveness doesn't mean that you deny the other person's responsibility for hurting you, and it doesn't minimize or justify the wrong. You can forgive the person without excusing the act. Forgiveness brings a kind of peace that helps you go on with life. [4]

I forgave and even thought I had to learn how to forget about most of the things that took place in my situation. That's easier said than done, but it's something I grew to do. I was daily seeking God's love for my life and applying the scripture Isaiah 43:18-19: "Remember not the former things, nor consider the things of old. Behold, I am doing a new thing; now it springs forth, do you not perceive it? I will make a way in the wilderness and rivers in the desert." I found that with God being the One whom I trusted, He was doing something new in my life and now I'm still alive to talk about it. My life was free because of Him.

Even though I forgave that person that I didn't know, I had to love him in spite of the situation. As crazy as it may sound, I love the person who did this to me. I don't love what they did, but I grew to love them because God said so. Matthew 22: 39 says you must "Love your neighbor as yourself." How to show the love of Christ is one of the main things I've learned throughout this process. No it wasn't easy, but over time I made it.

I came out of that phase where I withdrew myself from the world and others around me who wanted to support me. I found trust, love, and forgiveness again. I thank God for my twin brother who never gave up on me and continually encouraged me to begin using my gifts again.

CHAPTER ELEVEN

DRIVEN BY PURPOSE

My twin brother Marcus was instrumental in pushing me to reconnect with my purpose. Around the time of my incident, Marcus was getting ready to release his album called *Now* and he wanted me to sing on it so he held it up until I came home after my incident. I actually recorded one of the songs on his album with a tube in my stomach and my ostomy bag. Throughout the time I was singing the song you could hear all of my emotions. I was crying; I was nervous; I was scared. I actually thought I wasn't going to be able to sing again after what happened to me, so to know that I could still sing was shocking. It was surreal. I was emotionally unhinged, like "Wow God, You allowed me to live and now that I know I can still sing, I am going to sing a lot more now."

Marcus' song was phenomenal and I was able to dig a little deeper. It actually released a new sound in me. Everyone tells me my voice is totally different now, that it's more meaningful, like a new sound was birthed within me from my situation. I was able to reach deeper inside myself and sing with a passion and hunger to deliver and to break certain things in the spirit realm.

I began to write new songs. I had already started to write songs for my album, but I ended up rewriting a lot of them after what happened because I felt like they were not me anymore. So much new music came out of my situation.

Many times I would be crying while I was writing the songs, yelling, contemplating doing things that are un-characteristic of me, and praying, "God only you can help me do this; I need you God, I hear You, I want to make you happy, I want to please you – I don't want to do anything that's contrary to Your Word."

You can actually hear the emotions in the music. For example, with my song, *Free in the Garden*, I receive a lot of testimonials about how it ministers to people, how they become free after hearing it. When I wrote it I felt like I was stuck in a mindset, stuck in a disturbing situa-tion, stuck in captivity, stuck in danger, stuck in a place where the enemy tries to keep you, but I realized that God Himself came as the ultimate sacrifice, the atone-ment to free us from that. Before I understood that I kept feeling like I wouldn't be able to get out of that mindset. I had to free myself. This song was inspired by "the gar-den" because of the image that Satan painted for Adam and Eve which caused them to deviate from God's assignment for their lives (Genesis 3).

I had to keep reminding myself, "No, no, the devil is a liar, I'm free from that, I'm free from that, I'm free from that. I'm free in the garden." I said, "No longer will I be bound to that, that's crazy, the enemy is not going to keep painting pictures in my mind, making me think that someone is going to come and kill me. They can do whatever they will, but nothing is going to keep me from continuing to be driven by my purpose. It's not going to stop me from being purposed to live."

I'm thankful that Jesus Christ shed His blood for me and I know that's why I'm still alive, why I'm still here. I identified with Him, that what I went through is a sacrifice for something greater. Jesus didn't just die, He rose, and He is still standing. I am still living, I'm still standing. I can't totally understand everything about my life, but I know there is a strong purpose for my life and I know there is more inside of me. I need to drive my true purpose more.

> How often do you think about your purpose in life? Have you ever asked yourself the question, "What is my ultimate purpose on Earth?" What is driving you to be here today? Knowing God's purpose for your life is the most essential thing you can ever imagine. God already knows the purpose and plans for your life.

> *"'For I know the plans I have for you,' declared the Lord, 'plans to prosper you and not to harm you, plans to give you hope and a future.'" Jeremiah 29:11*

God has given you the opportunity to move forward in His plans, but you must learn how to identify and recognize what those true plans are for your life. It's so important that you keep reading His Word and connect your heart to Him daily. God looks at our inner selves and man looks at the outer (1 Samuel 16:7).God looks at the motives behind what we speak. His true purpose for us is that we love Him with all of our heart, soul and mind, then love our neighbors as we love ourselves (Matthew 22:37-38).

Those are the most important commandments that should drive our purpose for living. Those two commandments are the driving forces in helping us move to that place God wants us to be in. What is driving you right now? Do you have your car in park or do you have it cranked up and ready to go? God didn't create us in His image for no reason. He didn't design us to sit and wait on Him. We have to put our cars in gear and get started with His assignment and purpose. God is not going to harm you. He is not going to put too much on you than you can bear. Trust me, I know.

I thought at one point He was putting too much on me, until I finally realized that He was preparing me. I had to believe it. I had to walk in it. We have to take time out of our so-called busy day and stay connected with

God on a personal level in order to truly understand what direction He wants us to drive in. God knew who we were even before the foundations of this earth, and today it's our responsibility to connect to Him and gain confidence in Him so we can move to where He wants us to be.

God tells us in Jeremiah 1:5: "Before I formed you in the womb I knew you, before you were born I set you apart; I appointed you as a prophet to the nations." This scripture helps us understand that God has always been with us and He already knew how important we were going to be in this world. Today is your day to recognize and identify what your true self looks like. There is so much more that can be pulled out of you right now. I'm still going places I've never been before. I'm excited because I know I will meet you there. We will get there together. Keep driving and take the time to get into that realm where God is. Let God lead and drive you down the path of righteousness. You are purposed to live, so live on purpose.

The devil tried to harm me, but God shielded me! God is the true protector and comforter for your life. I tried Him for myself and He's all right. Oh yeah, He's cool like that. That's the God I know and serve. I know I'm purposed to live because ever since I was very young, I knew God placed something special on the inside of me. I knew there was more work I needed to complete and singing was just one of the things I enjoyed doing.

I could never forget about my start as a singer and how it brought me to this point. I always wanted to record a CD and saw myself traveling the world, but I never knew how it was going to happen. I just knew I had to keep pushing. I had to keep driving because God has purposed me for this journey.

I have always had the feeling that you get when you want something so badly that you just can't let it go. That feeling seems to get stronger as time goes by. I needed more in my life and I felt like it couldn't happen fast enough. However, I just constantly stayed focused even in the midst of all the many storms and headaches I have experienced. My main motivation has always been to pursue the passions and purpose God placed inside me.

Earlier in this chapter I talked about the sound that came forth when I started recorded the song for my twin brother's album. When I left the hospital and came back into Corner's Studio, I realized I never thought I would see a studio again. I never imagined that my life would cause me to transition back to doing what I love to do. I never thought my vocal ability would even be the same, but there was something that kept me from stopping. For one, my brother kept encouraging me to keep pushing. "I know you can do it," he said. So I did it. I started recording. Why, because he not only pushed me, but he reminded me of my true purpose. Because I was still living, I was able to sing on the track for his album. That was a driving force for me.

My Lord, it was a good feeling. I felt something far greater than passion come through my vocal cords. It's like a sensation that can't be described. The song was called *Together Forever* and as I thought about the song, it made me realize that God was telling me how we were always together. He stayed true to His Word and He wanted me to stay true to mine as well. "Just stay close and I will never leave or forsake you Marcel."

I knew because God and I were together, nothing in the world could stop me from moving into the next level of my life. The sound was so new and fresh for my life. I reached deeper inside myself than ever before. I closed my eyes and pictured myself in the clouds, just me and my musical gift.

Sometimes you have to block those distractions of life that get in the way of your purpose. You just have to connect with your passion or that gift living on the inside of you in order to get to the place God is intending you to go. Once I finished that song, I knew I felt different. I knew my sound would never be the same. I could feel a sense of freedom. It was that simple release of emotions that allowed me to let go and not worry about who was around me. Don't worry so much about what is not happening. Matthew 6:34 says, "Therefore do not worry about tomorrow, for tomorrow will worry about itself. Each day has enough trouble of its own." That should be your driving force.

Today you may be worrying about how you can drive in your purpose. Don't let any worry or doubt get in the way. Drive safely enough so nothing will get in the way of your final destination. Why? You are driven by purpose.

What are you purposed to do? List three things you are purposed to do on earth:

_____

_____

_____

Are you exercising your God-given purpose? If not, what is holding you back?

_____

_____

_____

_____

_____

_____

_____

_____

_____

_____

_____

CHAPTER TWELVE

TRANSITION

> What is Transition? The process or a period of changing from one state or condition to another. (Merriam Webster Dictionary)

Seven in all but one has Transitioned

Growing up with six siblings was a joy. I have three brothers and three sisters and I'm the next to youngest of all seven. My mother had two sets of twin boys. "The Anderson Twins" are what people used to call the four of us. Growing up in the church, we sang all over for different community and church events. My brothers and I would wear the usual, white shirts, black bowties and black pants. Thank God for my mother dressing us in the simplest colors. As we became older, we began to branch off into our own personal gifts. We all had some unique gifts on the inside and we never stopped digging deeper for what those were. Given many opportunities in life, we went after what was presented to us. Thank God for parents who allowed us to be involved in the right things. Not everyone is fortunate enough to have those types of opportunities. Even though we would fuss and fight throughout our process of discovery, we always supported each other and gave each other encouraging words that helped us find the secret gifts buried on the inside of us. We did that for each other until we became old enough to realize that we all had a purpose for which to live. We all had dreams for the future and aspirations for the present, but one of my siblings' dreams was stopped by a tragic accident.

A Tragic Situation

It was a sunny day on November 28, 2012 when I received a phone call from my mother while I was teaching some high school students. Normally, I would ignore my calls while I was teaching, but for some reason, I had to take this call and ask my mother what was going on. "Is everything ok?" I asked. "No," she said and then explained that Aaron, my older brother who is the twin of Alphaeus, had been in a car accident and the police were not telling her anything. "Pray," she said. "Really mamma?" I asked. "What happened to him?" 'Click.' The phone hung up and I began to pray to myself. Something came over me that didn't feel too good. I didn't know what to expect. I gathered my thoughts and continued to pray out loud, steadily walking towards the baseball field of the high school. I couldn't go back into the classroom. I wasn't feeling it right then. I had to get some answers. I started calling my family members and no one would pick up the phone.

Finally I got in contact with one of my siblings and they said Aaron was taken to the emergency room. All I could do is think about what could have happened and if he was alright. I prayed like my mother said, but I still couldn't get that feeling off my back. Have you ever received some troubling news and you were asked to pray, but for some reason during your prayer, it didn't feel like your prayer was getting to that place you wanted it to? That's how I felt. At that moment, I just couldn't shake the feeling off my back. When I finally learned the details of Aaron's condition, it was worse than I imagined.

In a major car accident, a man had hit my brother's car, causing it to flip off the road. Aaron was now in ICU because he had eight broken ribs and a bruised lung with several severe wounds throughout his body. He was fighting for his life, but I knew he would walk away from the situation.

From the first moment I received a call that something happened to him all I could think about was how he responded when I was hurt. When I was in the hospital and Aaron received the call about me being robbed, he was the first one who made it to North Carolina from South Carolina. He was the most concerned at that moment. My mother told me he reacted in a very unusual way, adding layers of clothing as he was preparing to get to where I was. "Man," I said to myself. "Lord help my brother make it through this. Please help him. Just help him make it through this."

The Hospital Visit

As I finally arrived at the hospital, I walked into the waiting room and saw my mother and father sitting there with a peculiar look on their faces. They were concerned about their son who was still in ICU fighting for his life and all they could do was wait, pray, and be patient. Hmm, that's all we could do during our stay in the hospital. We waited, prayed, and continued to have patience with the doctors as they constantly gave us reports about Aaron's condition. Some were good and some were reports we dreaded to hear. All I could think was, "God is a healer." Thinking back to my situation, I said, "God is going to do the same thing for Aaron that He did for me." I was so confident in what I was saying and just knew my prayers would be answered.

As we continued to wait and pray, Aaron's condition began to get better, but he still had a long way to go. Looking at him lay there on his bed, I couldn't help but reflect back on my hospitalization at Duke Hospital. I saw myself as I looked at him and thought, "Aaron is a fighter and he will be just fine."

A week went by and I traveled back to work and constantly checked on Aaron's condition with my family. "He's getting a little better," my family said. "That's my boy," I told myself. "Aaron you were built to do this;" I hyped myself up as I received the updates over the phone. "I know you're going to get through this moment brother." Daily I received emails and phone calls from people who were praying and looking for updates about my brother's condition. "He's doing better but keep praying for him."

As we continued praying that my brother's condition would get better, something just kept pulling on my spirit and I couldn't tell what it was. Praying and waiting got me so twisted that I took to running to stay positively focused and remind myself that it was in God's hands. He was going to work this entire thing out for Aaron. Sometimes you have to put it in God's hands; God will work it out for you. Just moments after I returned from one of my long runs, I received another call from my family saying that Aaron had to be put on dialysis. All I could say was "Wow!" When I heard those words, all I could do was just sit and ponder what he was going through. "How is he really doing?" I thought to myself. I couldn't talk to him but I knew he was feeling everything that was happening to him, even though he was sedated. "God help Aaron," were my only other words at the time. In the midst of things getting better, it seemed that things were getting worse. Praying and waiting were the only things to do and that's what we did.

A day or so went by and another call came that Aaron's heart stopped and I didn't know what to say. I prayed and prayed and began to get upset that what I was praying for didn't seem to be happening. "Lord I'm praying and I'm trying to figure out what in the world is going on here." Have you ever felt that way before? You prayed and you cried; you cried and you prayed. I'm sure you have. If you ever had someone fighting on their death bed, I'm sure it kept you up all night wondering how they would get through.

I couldn't take it anymore. I finally got back on the road and started heading back towards Spartanburg Regional Hospital to be with Aaron and my family. I was going to go pray and lay hands on my brother. I needed him to come out of that ICU room. While on the road, I called my Pastor at the time, B. McKinley Bayless and we prayed and declared that Aaron was going to be OK. I was mad, upset, angry, and all the above, but I knew I had to get my spirit right in order to deliver an effective prayer over his life. When I arrived after a three hour drive from NC, I walked into the hospital to a room full of friends and family members whose facial expressions resembled a distant stare. Some were crying and some were praying for the situation to get better for Aaron. "How is it going?" I asked. "His heart is working again and they are watching and monitoring him closely. The doctor is constantly checking his heart and they are doing everything they can to make sure he gets better."

It was late and I knew I was tired, but I charged towards the back where my brother Aaron was. As I began examining the hospital environment and the nurses around him, I started to engage in more prayer as I cried internally. Still reflecting back to my hospitalization, I just knew he would get up soon and walk away from this situation. I knew Aaron was a fighter. The next day went by and results were showing that Aaron was getting better even after his heart stopped twice.

I went back to NC and I felt good again until I received a call two days later. "Aaron's heart has stopped again and it's not looking too good."

Prayer was the only thing I could think of at that moment. I starting calling my family but they were all with the doctor so they were not picking up. I didn't know what to think; my mind went blank. I was calling and no one was picking up the second time. I was praying and Marcus, my twin was in the back room waiting just like me to hear the results. "No," I said. "It's not true. Stop playing. It's not happening like that. Keep praying," I said. "Keep working on him." Alphaeus, Aaron's twin was constantly talking to me through text messaging, letting me know that they were still working on Aaron's heart. They worked on him for at least an hour but he didn't respond. At that moment, I knew it wasn't looking too good for my family and especially Aaron. "No," I said to myself. "No. God, you still can work this out for Aaron." It didn't happen the way I wanted it to. My brother transitioned from earth. I didn't understand and I couldn't put the pieces together.

Again thinking back to my own incident, I asked myself, "Why?" As I pondered why things had to end this way, I realized that God is still God in the midst of tragic situations. Yet as people, we may not always understand or have the answers to our problems. That doesn't mean we have to blame God for every situation we can't control or understand. God is the same yesterday, today, and tomorrow. He is a loving God who wants to see everyone transition into the kingdom. However we have to learn how to carry out His plans for our life in order for that to happen. This earth is not our home and we must learn to prepare for the transitioning phase of life.

No man knows the day or the hour when God will appear. We don't even know when we will take our last breath. We must make sure our life is lining up with His Word so we can live with Him for eternity. When my incident took place, at first I didn't understand why it happened to me, but through processing my situation and talking to God, I found myself connecting back to a place of security in Him daily. I found security in God because I realized that He was still my shelter even though someone invaded my space and tried to take my life and my identity.

My brother has transitioned to live with God and I know without a doubt that I will transition to Heaven one day and see him again, face-to-face.

Aaron's Influence

As a young boy, I was especially influenced by the example of my older brothers and ever since I was in middle school, I've looked up to my brother Aaron in many different ways. When I started playing sports, Aaron was the driving force in why I wanted to participate in track and field especially. I remember when he would come home from track practice and run hurdles outside our house. "He's practicing every day to get better," I thought to myself. "That's something I could do." So I did. I tried it out.

Playing around outside when no one was looking, I jumped the hurdle with no form or technique. My Lord, I almost busted my rear end. As I got back up, I said to myself, "I'm not sure about this." Within the next year or two, I decided to run track after my basketball season at Dorman High School in Spartanburg, SC. My brother led the way during that track season.

Coach Urban was looking for new talent so every new athlete had to run a 400 meter race. I began to run as fast as I could, not really knowing what I was doing. I had no technique, form or anything, I just ran like Forrest Gump. All I could hear in the background was, "Run Marcel, and put your head down." Running like "Who shot John," I didn't want to lose to the guys beside me. My brother screamed from the top of his lungs, "Run man, you got this. Just keep your head down." While I was running I didn't know how I was doing, but after it was over I realized I had just won the race. Jumping up and down with excitement, my brother Aaron recruited me for their 4x4 relay.

During practice I always wondered when I would see my brother jump those hurdles again. One day I asked Aaron to teach me how to run hurdles, thinking it couldn't be that hard. I didn't tell him I almost busted my butt when I tried it at home. As we started setting up the hurdles for my first time during practice, he challenged me to jump. I was a little nervous this time. People were watching, my brother was watching, but I knew this was something I wanted to try out. I did it. Aaron started helping me to become better at running and jumping the hurdles and I felt good about track. It gave me a drive to push through challenges on and off the track. Even when I fell, I had no choice but to get back up again. I knew I had to show my brother that I wasn't a quitter.

With the help of my brother's leadership on the track, I received a scholarship to run track in college. Never giving up, I continued to work hard and receive numerous awards in all conference, state, and national championships. When I went to college I also chose the same degree as Aaron. Studying psychology and special education gave me the opportunity to connect with him even more. He was a teacher and I became one. The list goes on and on when it comes to how Aaron influenced me in the pursuit of my purpose.

The ultimate thing I enjoyed most about my brother's influence was that he never gave up on his dreams and aspirations. He always kept going in spite of the challenges in life. Because he pushed me in so many areas, I'm driven by purpose. I'm motivated daily to carry on some of the things he left on this earth to do. I channel my energy towards things that will bring change within the community of young people across the world, especially young men. I'm driven to lead young men within my organization, Accelerating Men to identify and understand who they are. My brother Aaron helped me define my organization when he was living on earth and he continues to motivate me even now that he's transitioned to Heaven.

A Better Place when you Transition

Will you get to see God and your loved ones when you transition? Today you have to answer that question. Do you know God for yourself? Have you heard about Jesus? If not, I encourage you to get to know Him. Learn more through picking up the Bible for yourself and learn to trust in Him. God will lead you in the right direction. He will never leave you nor forsake you. Everlasting life is for real and we all end up going somewhere after death. The question is, where will you transition to?

I'm sure at one point in your life you may have feared death. If not, you are among many people who don't or haven't thought too much about it. Over time you understand that it is part of this process called life. However, I know at one point in my life I feared death so much that I wanted to live as long as I could to avoid it. All I could think about is living on this earth and enjoying what God placed in it: food, cars, family, trees, opportunity, traveling, vacation, education, ministry and so much that we all enjoy. But how long will we be able to enjoy it all? How long will this life last on earth? Will there be a day when we have to leave it all behind us? No matter how hard I think about it, one day I will die. We will all die and transition to another place. As a Christian man I learned that we are all given the opportunity to choose where we will transition to.

There are two places we could end up in when we transition from this earth: Heaven or Hell. Yes, these are two real places. It's something to think about. Heaven is the place where God is and Hell is being separated from God. Don't be separated from Him before you transition from earth. He loves you and wants nothing but the best for you. He wants you to accept Him as your Savior today. In order for us to get to Heaven, we have to align our lives with the way Jesus lived His life. When we accept Jesus as Savior, our lives change as we apply His commandments daily. It is part of our preparation for Heaven, the place where God lives and where His Son Jesus is sitting, right there on the right side of His Father, interceding on our behalf. This is the place where we will meet our Heavenly Father face-to-face and hope to hear Him say, "Well done thou good and faithful servant."

Heaven is a place where there is no sickness, pain, heartache, sorrow, disease, or violent killing. Meet me there! I recognize you may not be a believer in Jesus, but I encourage you to learn more about Him. I know that during my assault He was the main one who helped me get through it all. He allowed me to get to know Him in a very intimate way. He covered and sheltered me with His love, a special love that no person in this entire world could ever give me.

If your heart is broken, He can mend it. If your mind needs to be fixed, He can transform it with His words over you. If your body is wounded, know that you can be healed because God is a healer. While I was in the hospital, I wrote a song called *He's a Healer*, which is on my first album, *Still Living*. I wrote it when I read Isaiah 53, "But he was pierced for our transgressions, he was crushed for our iniquities: the punishment that brought peace was upon him and by his wounds we are healed." We have to trust and believe those words in order to receive God's healing; that's what I did. I knew it wasn't my time to die on earth and I became more confident in Him when I wrote and sang that song to myself.

Question for you today: has it ever been on your mind about when you are going to die and how you are going to die? If you ever felt like you were going to die and it seemed like you had so much more to give, how did you feel? I know I wanted to cry when I thought I couldn't put my hand to the plow anymore. My life was flashing before me, but I'm *Still Living*, because God loves me.

"Whatever you do, do it with all your might, for when you go to the grave, there will be no work or planning or knowledge or wisdom" (Ecclesiastes 9:10). Today we all have so much work to do before we transition to the next place after earth. There is so much more in you that is waiting to come out, but you have to be willing to put your hands to work. Even if you feel like there's nothing left inside of you to do, I encourage you to keep flying high within yourself and find your purpose, because there is more in you. The opportunity for you to say your last goodbyes and tell your last minute jokes to your friends has not presented itself yet. Why? Because if you are reading my words right now that means you are *Still Living*. There is still time for you to live out your dreams and vision. Just write out the vision and make a plan.

> *"For God so loved the World that He gave His only begotten Son that whosoever believes in Him shall not perish but have everlasting life." John 3:16*

NOW LIVE

With so many challenges that life can bring, it can also bring joy, happiness, peace, love, and so much more once you understand your purpose for living. Tomorrow is never promised and you will die one day; I just hope you know where your spirit will end up when you leave this earth. Until that day approaches, there's so much more inside of you that has to come out.

Reach a little deeper and grab the real you. I want you to know that God has predestined you for greatness today. Don't stop yourself from reaching towards your destination. Never let anything or anyone keep you from following your dreams and visions in life. No matter how bad your situation may be, you have to keep pressing on, in spite of the adversity.

Today is a new day and tomorrow is not here. Therefore, you have time to tap into that next level of faith and keep it moving. Without faith it's impossible to please God, and without God it's impossible to live the right kind of life. The minute you want to throw in the towel and quit, look into the mirror and tell yourself, "I'm more than a conqueror."

If you are facing a tough time in your life, you can find safety in Jesus. He's the Savior of the world and no one else could have helped me in my situation but Him. I hope you know that you can seek Him, learn more about who He is, and never walk away from Him. Jesus' story helped me and I hope my story caused you to think about who you are and what you are called to do. What are you doing with your life? If you're still living, that means you are purposed to live.

After reading this book, I hope you understand how important you are to God's kingdom. I hope you learn how to develop a closer walk with Jesus as you prepare to transition from this earth. I hope you continue to move forward in every area of your life. I hope that you search deeper within your personal situation and release that internal voice that's been closed up inside you for years. I hope you learn how to speak up and never let those around you keep you from making the right decisions for your life. I pray you learn how to forgive those who have hurt you. Don't keep those grudges inside for too long before they explode. Let it go and Let God have His way. It feels better and you will be rewarded for being obedient to the Holy Spirit. I pray that through the Holy Spirit, your life will be guided and many windows of opportunity will be available for you.

You are purposed to live!

Sources

1. http://www.ostomy.org/ostomy_info/whatis.html
2. http://www.ncadv.org/files/MaleVictims.pdf
3. http://www.ncadv.org/files/MaleVictims.pdf
4. http://www.mayoclinic.org

REFLECTIONS

Honoring my Brother
Dr. Aaron T. Anderson
(aka Mr. Table Talk)

You may have never heard of Dr. Aaron T. Anderson, also known as Mr. Table Talk. My brother was one of the most influential persons I know. Many people have spoken about how much he encouraged and inspired them to become more than what they thought they could be. People still talk about how much they enjoyed his table talk discussions and long, drawn-out lectures.

That's Dr. Aaron Anderson for you. Aaron was a talker. He would talk your head off about things you never even heard about, and after you left that table talk, you knew a little more than before. Dr. Aaron Anderson was more than just a brother to my siblings and me. He was a kindhearted person and track coach who would go far beyond to get you what you asked for. He would scream, fuss, yell or even say no at times, but he would call back later and say, "All right, man. I got ya."

He was the brother that many could call on and seek advice, wisdom, knowledge, and of course guidance. He received his Master's degree as a counselor and was highly qualified to do what God called Him to do. The countless conversations he had with people on a daily basis left them blessed and inspired by his words. His many inspirational social media messages kept his audience wondering what he would post next. Dr. Aaron Anderson used motivational words to change the world. He was a life-changer. He used electrifying words to transform the minds of unchanged personalities. He helped people heal by causing them to listen and think. He drove positive thinking and he was moving to another level. My God, he was on to something big. He wanted to become a doctor and was preparing to join a doctoral program. That's why you see Dr. in front of his name; I made him an honorary doctor. He deserves it.

Aaron wanted nothing but the best for everyone. He was the type of brother who understood what it took to keep a family strong and constantly made sure your mind was full of something good (a good book to read that is). [Our Uncle Nigel D. Alston and Cousin Anthony Wheeler opened the door for us to read more. Uncle Nigel also encouraged us to dig deeper than before to find out who we really were. Thank you for inspiring Aaron and all of us.]

Dr. Aaron T. Anderson will never be forgotten for all of his great accomplishments on earth. Heaven received a great spirit in 2012 and I know they are rejoicing daily with him. His spirit is *Still Living*.

I'm sure we all have had some hard and long crying nights about a loved one before, but I'm thankful to know that my moments were spent reflecting on someone special. Dr. Aaron, we miss you man, and we love you. Your spirit still lives on. I know every year is another year to work harder, as we continue to remember your incredible life here on earth. God is good and I'm thankful to know just that. Until we meet again, Phi Nu, this book is dedicated to you.

Words from Aaron's Mind

"The ability to become a man starts with the ability to understand responsibility. A man's number one responsibility is to understand himself. For me to do this is to know God and be in conversation with my mother."

"The first step in the acquisition of wisdom is silence. The second is listening. The third is memory. The fourth is practice a lot. And fifth is teaching."

"You will never go beyond your excuses."

"A grown man with a childlike mentality won't make it far. In order to change, change your situation, change your environment, your friends, your actions, but first you have to change your mind..."

Poem by Dr. Aaron T. Anderson

Who I am Finally Free

Waking from a deep sleep of reality, agony. Sitting on the side of the bed, wondering how I got caught up in this. I'm imprisoned by my mind; wasting time, focused on things that I may never see. Finally I'm Free. Free to see more than just some perfect world or just some make believe. Lesson of give, give all you got, one day at a time, instead of trying to figure life out. Finally I'm Free. Give it to me, cause I'm ready to give, give nothing less, far above and beyond some mess, who was I trying to impress, this ain't no contest. I just want to bless you for helping me find me.

Aaron's Words live on in this Book.

DISCUSSION QUESTIONS

1. What makes you a man or a woman? What gives you your identity?

2. Who is your support system?

3. What do you do to help you deal with negative thoughts from something you have experienced?

4. What makes you feel like you don't want to talk about your situation?

5. What would motivate you to speak up?

6. What outcomes do you expect from speaking about your story?

7. Why should someone else speak up?

8. What are the benefits of forgiving the person(s) who have done you wrong?

9. What gifts and talents do you have?

10. Are you confident about what will happen when you transition from this life?

11. Do you have a personal relationship with Jesus Christ?

12. What drives you and motivates you to move forward in life?

REFLECTIONS

GIVING UP IS NOT AN OPTION

An Honest Prayer

"Devil you thought you had me. You tried to kill me. Knocking at my door daily, you definitely tried your best to get me to slip up in my relationship with God. Hmmm… nice attempt, but I'm not going to let you get to me. I'm not going to let you mess with my mind today. I'm not giving up on myself anymore. I was bought with a price. Jesus paid it all for me and I'm glad about it. So God, I come before you again in need of Your help, because I'm not going to give up on me."

Giving Up is Not an Option

New Year's resolution was written, my goals were plain, and the execution was clear. I was going to finish my CD and begin to shape the foundation of my ministry, but things took a drastic change. One evening I was helping someone move when my life flashed before my eyes. Held at gunpoint, I had a decision to make. Should I lose hope and give up or stay strong and believe that I would live? I chose to keep hope. The same glimpse of hope and faith I got that night is the same hope and faith that I operate on today. Trusting in the Lord daily with all of your heart is something you must do so that you do not give up. I know that God is willing to us lead us in the right direction as we lean on Him to help us make sound decisions.

Proverbs 3:5-6 says "Trust in the LORD with all thine heart; and lean not unto thine own understanding. In all thy ways acknowledge him, and he shall direct thy paths." (KJV)

We all face the struggles and obstacles of life differently. There are always multiple options but there is always one option that tries to work itself into the equation, which is, giving up. To give up is to abort, stop, or hinder something before its completion. Giving up looks rather attractive when things become difficult. This is what the principalities of evil desire, for the kingdom of God to become stagnant and irrelevant. But we all know that God has commissioned us to advance His kingdom using our gifts. Giving up is not an option when you know that you were born with a purpose. God has ordained every individual on earth with a special gift inside them.

During Christmastime, can you remember when your parents wanted you to open your gifts, because they were excited about what was inside? They knew they had worked so hard to get you something that would make you happy. God is doing the same thing. What is your gift and have you unwrapped it? Have you had the opportunity to shake it and discern what it is? Will you share it with someone else? God is waiting and looking to see if you will open the gift that He planted inside of you or if you will throw it away. "Before I formed you in the womb, I knew you before you were born, I set you apart. I appointed you as a prophet to the nations." (Jeremiah 1:5 NIV).

The gifts and huge dreams that God has given you take great laboring. We must be equipped to work hard to reach them every single day of our lives. We must keep going, even "if others don't appreciate your journey," as my friend Jossalyn would say. It is definitely your life to live and not theirs, so you have to constantly believe in yourself that you are capable of achieving great success and that nothing will stand in your way. Have you ever given up on believing that God would assist you? Even though sometimes we may feel wedged in a situation, we must understand that God can change our lives overnight if we do not give up.

Giving up should not be an option today. Though life can get you down at times, you have to hold on to God and keep the faith. You should never let go of His hand. Jesus even experienced struggle as He walked the earth. He said in John 16:33, "These things I have spoken unto you, that in me ye might have peace. In the world ye shall have tribulation: but be of good cheer; I have overcome the world." (KJV) Jesus had the option to give up, but He didn't. He knew the importance of His assignment and never gave up on His cross, so why should we? He warned us about crosses. He did not bear His alone, and He will not leave us to bear ours alone. We have Him to help us, so, don't give up!

REFLECTIONS

DON'T LOSE YOUR MIND

Do any of you remember these lyrics of a song by an artist named DMX: "Ya'll gonna make me lose my mind, up in here, up in here?" If you don't remember this song, it's an old school throwback. Have you ever felt like you were going to lose your mind through a tough situation or circumstance? Have you ever felt like no one would truly understand what you were thinking, even if they thought they knew what was going on in your mind? If they only knew how the neurotransmitters really worked in your brain! I only say this because no one will fully understand everything that goes on in our mind but God Himself. Since that is the case, it's important to consult with God when our mind begins to stray from His will in this life.

Our request to you Lord: "We need your guidance in our mind today and every day. We can't make it on our own. We don't understand everything Lord, but we still trust in your Word. Help us to take on your Spirit and characteristics when we can't comprehend many things in our minds."

We must continue to understand that the mind is powerful and it's a "terrible thing to waste." I pray that we keep our minds focused as much as possible on God even through the good times, so when something terrible happens in our life, we won't lose our minds "up in here, up in here" (DMX). The mind is considered to be the element or complex of elements in an individual that feels, perceives, thinks, wills, and especially reasons. Colossians 3:2 says, "Set your minds on things that are above, not on things that are on earth." This means that we must truly keep our minds in tune with the Spirit daily in order to understand what happens in the natural.

Every single day as true Christians, we must continue to exercise and condition our minds with the Spirit of God. My prayer for us today, is to allow the Holy Spirit to lead us in our conscious decisions. As we continue to reason and think about the daily events that happen at work, school, in our families, and especially in our own lives, let's keep our minds on the things which are above (heaven) before we lose our minds like DMX said in his song. Just remember this world is not our home.

About the Author

MARCEL ANDERSON

With an energetic, yet insightful and charismatic speaking style and a passion for all people, Marcel Anderson is a sought after revivalist and mentor who is called to empower and encourage individuals around the world. Dedicated to spreading the good news of the Gospel to everyone he meets, he has travelled throughout the country speaking to young people about knowing who they are and the importance of identifying their gifts.

A native of Spartanburg, South Carolina, Marcel graduated from Dorman High School. He went on to receive his Bachelor of Arts Degree in Psychology from Saint Augustine University in Raleigh, North Carolina and his ministerial license from St. Luke Ministerial Training. Marcel is currently finishing his Master of Arts degree in Social Psychology, and constantly makes use of his education and training to benefit the community.

In 2011, Marcel became the founder and CEO of Accelerating Men Inc., a nonprofit community faith-based organization that mentors young men ages 10-18. Through workshops, mentoring, and conference calls within North Carolina and South Carolina, Accelerating Men works hard to educate, train, and cultivate young men to become all that God has called them to be.

One of Marcel's greatest passions is singing. After being called to ministry, it was evident that Marcel would encourage the world through writing Gospel music with an irresistible R&B and Urban Soul contemporary groove. He got his start in writing and performing music with his three brothers in a group known as The Anderson Twins and was later part of a trio, Three Part Harmony.

When he launched his solo music career, Marcel Anderson's popularity quickly grew, as he allowed the spirit of God to be glorified through his music. It has been through the anointing and call on his life that he's been able to leave a long-lasting impression of worship on the lives he's touched. He has also been able to share the stage with local and national gospel greats such as Tye Tribbett, John P. Kee, Leandria Johnson, Shawn Bigby, and Teen Pure N Heart, which has helped to shape his future in Gospel music.

Marcel's freshmen project, *Still Living*, highlights some of the best producers in the jazz and gospel communities such as Nicholas Cole, Marcus Anderson, and Alphaeus Anderson. The project's theme surrounds his personal testimony and how he was able to triumph and overcome, giving believers new hope in Christ as his message proves that you can bounce back from the depths of life's most challenging events. The project was released in March 2014, accompanied by the release of his first book, entitled *Still Living: A Victimized Man's Journey*, in which he transparently shares his shocking, triumphant story of victory over death.

To book Marcel Anderson for your next event, workshop, conference or seminar, visit: http://www.marcelanderson.com/contact.

ACCELERATING MEN, INC.

MENTORING ORGANIZATION

ACCELERATING MEN, INC.

Who are we? A community faith-based organization with a devout responsibility to lead young men ages 10-18 to live a true lifestyle that reflects the will of God.

Vision: To provide a safe and trusting organization that makes a significant difference in the schools, churches, and community by providing constant change in the lives of young men.

Mission: To train young men to become all that God has called them to be and to encourage other men to do the same.

Educate, Train, Cultivate Monthly Workshops

Purpose of ETC Workshops- To help young men ages 10-18 identify who they truly are by introducing them to different types of community-life workshop topics, which will enrich and influence them during small group discussions, while encouraging, inspiring, and motivating them to become all that God has called them to be.

Get involved with Accelerating Men, Inc.

Visit: www.acceleratingmen.org to find out more.
Email: acceleratingmen@gmail.com

REFLECTIONS

Order Form

To order additional copies of this book and Marcel Anderson's CD, Still Living, indicate the number of copies you would like next to the title, provide your shipping address and contact information, enclose payment including shipping, and mail this form to:

Marcel Anderson/Rain Publishing
P.O. Box 702
Knightdale, NC 27545

Still Living, A Victimized Man's Journey $12.99 x____

Still Living, MA Music CD $9.99 x____

Shipping and Handling: $5.00

Total Enclosed: _____

Shipping Address:
Name: _____
Street: _____
City, State, Zip_____
Phone: _____
Email: _____

CPSIA information can be obtained
at www.ICGtesting.com
Printed in the USA
BVHW041014200920
589229BV00015B/774